Programming in Embedded C

Part - 1

Dedicated to My Daughter Saanvi Asthana and My Entire Family

About the Author:

I am Abhinandan Asthana and this book is the result of my involvement in Automotive Electronics, I have started my journey in Embedded Software and till now for past more than 8 years worked with Multiple Companies in the same domain.

Some of them are really big names in the industry. I have worked on Embedded C, AUTOSAR, CAN, LIN, SPI, Diagnostic Protocols KWP2000, UDS and many other protocols.

This book is based on the usage of Embedded C in Embedded Systems and in Automotive Electronics.

Hope it will help you in your Career Journey too.

Please mail your suggestions,

abhinandan.vns@gmail.com

Acknowledgements:

It's been 3 years when I have written my first book, people all over the world have purchased it. Even I have seen some people from Japan, Germany, US have purchased this book. Thanks to all of them first.

I want to acknowledge first My Parents – My Father (Shri. Krishna Mohan Asthana) and My Mother (Smt. Bindoo Asthana) for their efforts in teaching me and making me capable to do something on my own.

I want to acknowledge my younger brother (Abhinav Asthana) for being a helping hand whenever I need him.

I want to acknowledge My Wife (Remi Asthana) and My Loving Daughter (Saanvi Asthana) who are like my constant companion in my life journey.

Thanks to All for Supporting Me and Helping me in my endeavours.

Preface of First Edition:

This book will start with Introduction of Embedded C and how it's different from C Language. It covers basics of Embedded C along with emphasis on its usage in designing embedded software.

I have covered major topics such as Code Flow in Embedded C, Compilation process in Embedded C, Software Architecture.

Covered topics related to Real Time Operating Systems (RTOS), Interrupts, Storage Classes, Software Architecture.

In depth overview of processes involve in Build Process and various outputs at all levels.

Software Development Lifecycle in Embedded Systems.

Important Concepts and Questions frequently asked in Interviews.

Hope you like this book, please provide your valuable reviews.

Thank You!!

Best of Luck!!

Abhinandan Asthana

abhinandan.vns@gmail.com

Index:

1. What is Embedded C

Overview:

Looking around, we find ourselves to be surrounded by various types of embedded systems. Be it a digital camera or a mobile phone or a washing machine, all of them has some kind of processor functioning inside it.

Associated with each processor is the embedded software. If hardware forms the body of an embedded system, embedded processor acts as the brain, and embedded software forms its soul. It is the embedded software which primarily governs the functioning of embedded systems.

During infancy years of microprocessor-based systems, programs were developed using assemblers and fused into the EPROMs. There used to be no mechanism to find what the program was doing. LEDs, switches, etc. were used to check correct execution of the program. Some 'very fortunate' developers had In-circuit Simulators (ICEs), but they were too costly and were not quite reliable as well.

As time progressed, use of microprocessor-specific assembly-only as the programming language reduced and embedded systems moved onto C as the embedded programming language of choice. C is the most widely used programming language for embedded processors/controllers. Assembly is also used but mainly to implement those portions of the code where very high timing accuracy, code size efficiency, etc. are prime requirements.

Initially C was developed by Kernighan and Ritchie to fit into the space of 8K and to write (portable) operating systems. Originally it was implemented on UNIX operating systems. As it was intended for operating systems development, it can manipulate memory addresses. Also, it allowed programmers to write very compact codes. This has given it the reputation as the language of choice for hackers too.

As assembly language programs are specific to a processor, assembly language didn't offer portability across systems. To overcome this disadvantage, several high-level languages, including C, came up.

Some other languages like PLM, Modula-2, Pascal, etc. also came but couldn't find wide acceptance. Amongst those, C got wide acceptance for not only embedded systems, but also for desktop applications.

Even though C might have lost its sheen as mainstream language for general purpose applications, it still is having a strong-hold in embedded programming. Due to the wide acceptance of C in the embedded systems, various kinds of support tools like compilers & cross-compilers, ICE, etc. came up and all this facilitated development of embedded systems using C.

Embedded C vs C:

Embedded systems programming is different from developing applications on a desktop computer.

Key characteristics of an embedded system, when compared to PCs, are as follows:

- Embedded devices have resource constraints (limited ROM, limited RAM, limited stack space, less processing power).
- Components used in embedded system and PCs are different; embedded systems typically use smaller, less power consuming components.
- Embedded systems are more tied to the hardware.

Two salient features of Embedded Programming are code speed and code size.

Code speed is governed by the processing power, timing constraints, whereas code size is governed by available program memory and use of programming language.

Goal of embedded system programming is to get maximum features in minimum space and minimum time.

Embedded systems are programmed using different type of languages:

- Machine Code
- Low level language, i.e., assembly
- High level language like C, C++, Java, Ada, etc.
- Application level language like Visual Basic, scripts, Access, etc.

Assembly language maps mnemonic words with the binary machine codes that the processor uses to code the instructions. Assembly language seems to be an obvious choice for programming embedded devices. However, use of assembly language is restricted to developing efficient codes in terms of size and speed. Also, assembly codes lead to higher software development costs and code portability is not there.

Developing small codes are not much of a problem, but large programs/projects become increasingly difficult to manage in assembly language. Finding good assembly programmers has also become difficult nowadays. Hence high-level languages are preferred for embedded systems programming.

Advantages of Embedded C:

- It is small and reasonably simpler to learn, understand, program and debug.
- C Compilers are available for almost all embedded devices in use today, and there is a large pool of experienced C programmers.
- Unlike assembly, C has advantage of processor-independence and is not specific to any particular microprocessor/ microcontroller or any system.
- This makes it convenient for a user to develop programs that can run on most of the systems.
- As C combines functionality of assembly language and features of high level languages, C is treated as a 'middle-level computer language' or 'high level assembly language'.
- It is fairly efficient
- It supports access to I/O and provides ease of management of large embedded projects.

Why Embedded C:

Many of above advantages are offered by other languages also, but what sets C apart from others like Pascal, FORTRAN, etc. is the fact that it is a middle level language.

- It provides direct hardware control without sacrificing benefits of high level languages.
- Compared to other high-level languages, C offers more flexibility because C is relatively small, structured language.
- It supports low-level bit-wise data manipulation.
- Compared to assembly language, C Code written is more reliable and scalable, more portable between different platforms (with some changes).
- Programs developed in C are much easier to understand, maintain and debug. Also, as they can be developed more quickly, codes written in C offers better productivity.

- C is based on the philosophy 'programmers know what they are doing, only the intentions are to be stated explicitly.
- It is easier to write good code in C & convert it to an efficient assembly code (using high quality compilers) rather than writing an efficient code in assembly itself.
- Benefits of assembly language programming over C are negligible when we compare the ease with which C programs are developed by programmers.

Objected oriented language, C++ is not apt for developing efficient programs in resource constrained environments like embedded devices. Virtual functions & exception handling of C++ are some specific features that are not efficient in terms of space and speed in embedded systems. Sometimes C++ is used only with very few features, very much as C.

Ada, also an object-oriented language, is different than C++. Originally designed by the U.S. DOD, it didn't gain popularity despite being accepted as an international standard twice (Ada83 and Ada95). However, Ada language has many features that would simplify embedded software development.

Java is another language used for embedded systems programming. It primarily finds usage in high-end mobile phones as it offers portability across systems and is also useful for browsing applications. Java programs require Java Virtual Machine (JVM), which consume lot of resources. Hence it is not used for smaller embedded devices.

Dynamic C and C# are some proprietary languages which are also being used in embedded applications.

Efficient embedded C programs must be kept small and efficient; they must be optimized for code speed and code size. Good understanding of processor architecture embedded C programming and debugging tools facilitate this.

2. Build Process and Build Environment

In this section we are going to discuss about the generic Build Process followed in C/C++ Programming and how Embedded C Build Process is different from that:

2.1 Generic Build Process

- When the C code runs there is four stages of C code building process which utilizes different 'tools' such as a pre-processor, compiler, assembler, and linker. Finally, we get executable/. hex file from .c file.
- Here are the stages which are involved in C code building process in order regardless of the operating system/compiler.

2.1.1 Pre-processing:

- Pre-processing is the first stage of any C code building. It processes include-files, conditional compilation instructions and macros. Here we get "make errors" if there is some issue regarding the include files/macros. If some include files/macros are missing than there is "make_errors" or such errors are called make errors. For example, #define my_dma_en, if this "my_dma_en" deifne is used without "#define my_dma_en", then there will be make error for "my_dma_en" as undefined "my_dma_en"

2.1.2 Compilation:

- Compilation is the second stage of any C code building. It takes the output of the preprocessor, and the source code, and generates assembler source code. On this stage .asm files generated. If there are syntactical errors in source code than such errors are called compilation error.

2.1.3 Assembly:

- Assembly is the third stage of C code building. It takes the assembly source code and produces an assembly listing with offsets. The assembler output is stored in an object file.In this process .obj made from .asm.

2.1.4 Linking:

- Linking is the final stage of C code building. It takes one or more object files or libraries as input and combines them to produce a single (usually executable) file. In this process .exe made from .obj.

- In UNIX/Linux, the executable or binary file doesn't have extension whereas in Windows the executables for example may have .exe, .com and .dll. similarly file extensions can be .o or .obj for object file and .s or .asm for assembly files.

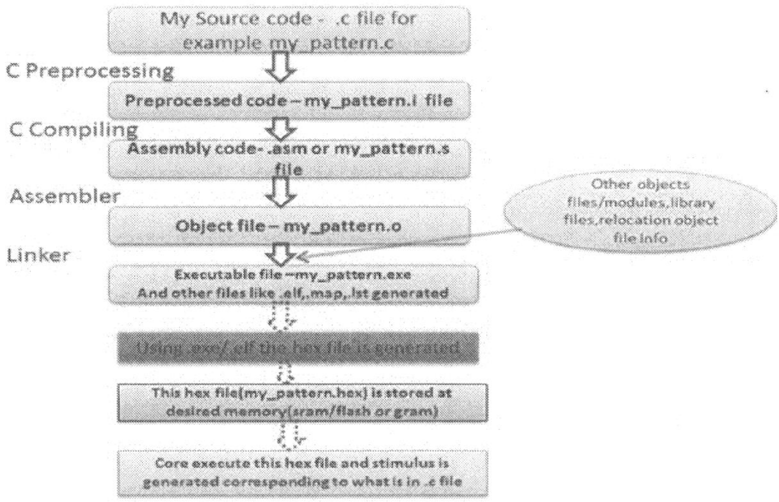

Figure 2.1 – Compilation Process

2.1.5 Object Files and Executables Files:

Assembler and linker generates the .obj or .o and .exe respectively. An object and executable come in several formats such as ELF (Executable and Linking Format) and COFF (Common Object-File Format) depending on OS .

An object file is basically a file containing machine language instructions and data in a form that the linker can use to create an executable program.

Each routine or data item defined in an object file has a corresponding symbol name by which it is referenced. A symbol generated for a routine or data definition can be either a local definition or global definition. Any reference to a symbol outside the object file is known as an external reference.

These object files have areas called sections. Sections can hold executable code, data, dynamic linking information, debugging data, symbol tables, relocation information, comments, string tables, and notes.

Some sections are loaded into the process image and some provide information needed in the building of a process image while still others are used only in linking object files. For example .txt section or .bss section.

By default, the format (.obj or .o) is unreadable format but can be made in .obj.txt format to make it readable format.

2.1.6 Object Files in Nut-shell – Fields in .o files:

.text: This section contains the executable instruction codes and is shared among every process running the same binary. This section usually has READ and EXECUTE permissions only. This section is the one most affected by optimization.

.bss: BSS stands for 'Block Started by Symbol'. It holds un-initialized global and static variables. Since the BSS only holds variables that don't have any values yet.

It doesn't actually need to store the image of these variables. The size that BSS will require at runtime is recorded in the object file, but the BSS (unlike the data section) doesn't take up any actual space in the object file.

.data: Contains the initialized global and static variables and their values. It is usually the largest part of the executable. It usually has READ/WRITE permissions.

.reloc: Stores the information required for relocating the image while loading.

2.2 More about File Formats:

Here we will talk more about the different file formats generated after the compilation of an Embedded C Program.

2.2.1 . elf:

(Executable and Linking Format) is binary format, which is used in Unix and Linux systems

For example: my_pattern.elf

```
ELF Header:
  Magic:   7f 45 4c 46 01 01 01 00 00 00 00 00 00 00 00 00
  Class:                             ELF32
  Data:                              2's complement, little endian
  Version:                           1 (current)
  OS/ABI:                            UNIX - System V
  ABI Version:                       0
  Type:                              EXEC (Executable file)
  Machine:                           ARM
  Version:                           0x1
  Entry point address:               0x19000000
  Start of program headers:          52 (bytes into file)
  Start of section headers:          387040 (bytes into file)
  Flags:                             0x5000002, has entry point, Version5 EABI
  Size of this header:               52 (bytes)
  Size of program headers:           32 (bytes)
  Number of program headers:         9
  Size of section headers:           40 (bytes)
  Number of section headers:         27
  Section header string table index: 24
```

```
Section Headers:
  [Nr] Name          Type          Addr     Off    Size   ES Flg Lk Inf Al
  [ 0]               NULL          00000000 000000 000000 00      0   0  0
  [ 1] .rom          PROGBITS      3ef00000 025580 000040 00  AX  0   0 16
  [ 2] .text         PROGBITS      19000000 000500 025080 00 WAX  0   0 256
  [ 3] .rodata       PROGBITS      3ef00040 0255c0 005430 00   A  0   0  4
  [ 4] .data         PROGBITS      3ef05470 02a9f0 000460 00  WA  0   0  4
  [ 5] .bss          NOBITS        3ef058d0 02ae50 0007c0 00  WA  0   0  4
  [ 6] .stack        NOBITS        3ef28000
```

```
Program Headers:
  Type      Offset   VirtAddr   PhysAddr   FileSiz MemSiz  Flg Align
  LOAD      0x000154 0x00000000 0x00000000 0x00020 0x00020 R   0x4
  LOAD      0x000174 0x00000800 0x00000800 0x00030 0x00030 R   0x4
  LOAD      0
```

```
Symbol table '.symtab' contains 362894 entries:
   Num:    Value  Size Type    Bind   Vis      Ndx Name
     0: 00000000     0 NOTYPE  LOCAL  DEFAULT  UND
     1: 3ef00000     0 SECTION LOCAL  DEFAULT    1
     2: 19000000     0 SECTION LOCAL  DEFAULT    2
     3: 3ef00040     0 SECTION LOCAL  DEFAULT    3
```

2.2.2 .hex:

In SoC setup,when C program runs, .exe/.elf is made after going through the C building processes i.e. making ->compiling and linking. In SoC setup this .exe/elf is converted into a formatted hex which is loaded at desired location (sram,flash or gram).

This ".hex " file is made so that,core can execute the hex from the desired location(sram,flash or gram).

In this hex, there is information embedded of the whole SoC environment (core files,all modules,C files and SoC setup files).

Therefore, In SoC environment, a "hex" file is generated from .elf/.exe. Core executes this hex file and stimulus corresponding to .C files is generated for modules in SoC setup.

The pattern.hex looks like:

```
@3ef00000 0000000000000000
@3ef00008 20ffe008600820aa
@3ef00010 48094906e0056008
@3ef00018 e7f6d0f428006800
@3ef00020 8000f3afbf00e7fe
@3ef00028 8000f3af8000f3af
@3ef00030 e7ed20003ef7f800
```

First column is the address of memory (sram, flash or gram) where hex is loaded address.

Above hex file in the format of address followed by data.

When a ".c" file runs in SoC setup ,the below files generated for each .c.

*.crt0.o, *.lst , .map, *.o, *.out, *.lnk, *.hex, *.srec

2.2.3 .map, .lst & .srec:

Map files contains the memory allocation details and addresses for each modules. And .lst gives the details for program counter movement for each piece of code and files/functions which are executed.

A symbol table is a look-up between symbol names and their addresses in memory. Compiler normally produces .lst file for the assembly code, and .map file with information about program and data memory usage.

A typical map file looks like: (this is for ARM core based SoCs)

```
Archive member included because of file (symbol)

./lib.Pattern_namea(exceptions.o)

                        .o (default_abort_handler)
./.Pattern_name.a(soc_api.o)
                        Pattern_name.o (enable_all_interrupts)

Allocating common symbols
Common symbol     size          file

access_BusMode    0x1           PATTERN_NAME.o
tea_counter       0x4           pattern_name.o
interrupt_number_router
                  0x4           pattern_name.o
gic_interrupt_number
                  0x4           pattern_name.o

Memory Configuration

Name          Origin          Length          Attributes
prom_vt       0x00016000      0x00001700
flash         0x19000000      0x00040000
tcraml        0x1fff8000      0x00008000
tcramu        0x1fff8000      0x00008000
ocram0        0x3ef00000      0x00024000
stack_ram     0x3ef28000      0x00002000
lc_row        0x18400200      0x00000100
-----
-----
Linker script and memory map

LOAD pattern_name.o
LOAD crt0.o
LOAD main.o
LOAD vectable.o
LOAD int_table.o
LOAD jump_cs0.o
LOAD status.o
              0x00000000              __SEC_ROM_START = 0x0
              0x00000000              __NORM_ROM_START = 0x0

.rom          0x3ef00000      0x40
 status.o(.text)
 .text        0x3ef00000      0x40 status.o
```

.lst looks like:

```
163    .equ SIZE_1K,     0x00000400
164    .equ SIZE_2K,     0x00000800
165    .equ SIZE_4K,     0x00001000
166    .equ SIZE_8K,     0x00002000
167    .equ SIZE_16K,    0x00004000
----
170    .equ SIZE_128K,   0x00020000
171    .equ SIZE_256K,   0x00040000
172    .equ SIZE_496K,   0x0007C000
173    .equ SIZE_508K,   0x0007F000
174    .equ SIZE_512K,   0x00080000
----
191    .equ SIZE_2G,     0x80000000
192    .equ EXT_MEM1,    0x20000000
193    .equ EXT_MEM2,    0x21000000
194
195
196    #.equ SIZE_72M, 0x04800000
197
198    #///////////////////////////////////////////////////////////////
199
200    #/BASE ADDRESSES
201
202    .equ SLAVE_0,     0x00000000
203    .equ SLAVE_0A,    0x00000000
204    .equ SLAVE_0B,    0x30000000
----
208    .equ SLAVE_1B,    0x1F800000
209    .equ SLAVE_1B1,   0x1E000000
---
--
398    .equ PROG_INT, (8)
399    .equ FPUNAVL_INT, (9)
400    .equ APUNAVL_INT, (10)
401    .equ DEC_INT, (11)
402    .equ FIT_INT, (12
----
```

.srec looks like:

```
S02B00002F70726F6A6563742F68616C6F5F312E305F76657269665F6E6F6261636B757031 2F7573722F756DF5
S3150000000002A517476EA56D4BC1453F47FEA36EFBC10
S315000000010CD9B7476EAE623BCFFFFFFFFFFFFFFFFFE1
S315000000800AF55AA05000000000000000191400020000
S3150000008104C0000001402001001000000000000045B
S31500000820FFFFFFFFFFFFFFFFFFFFFFFFFFFFFFFFFFFFFD2
------
```

2.3 Linking and Loading

Because there are various object files which are included as references to each others code and/or data, so various locations, these are combined during the link time.

2.3.1 Linking

After linking all of the object files together, the linker uses the relocation records to find all of the addresses that need to be filled in.

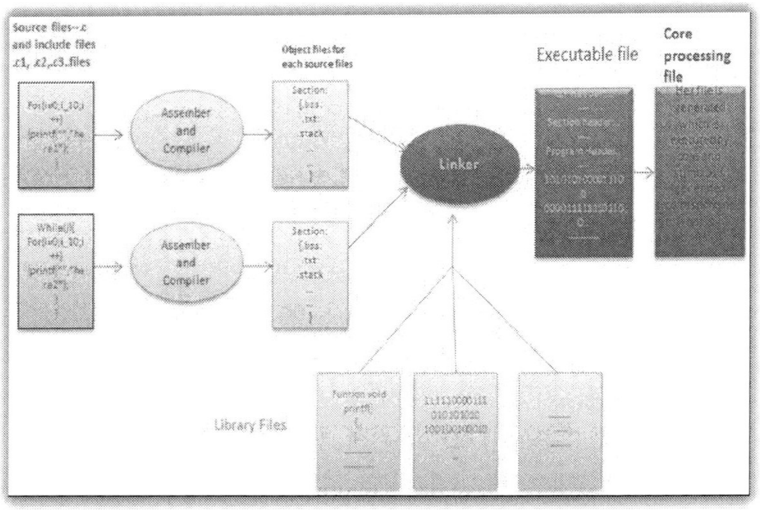

Figure 2.2 Linking

SHARED OBJECTS:

In a typical system, a number of programs will be running. Each program relies on a number of functions, some of which will be standard C library functions, like printf(), malloc(), strcpy(), etc. and some are non-standard or user defined functions.

If every program uses the standard C library, it means that each program would normally have a unique copy of this particular library present within it. This result in wasted resources, degrade the efficiency and performance. So it is better to have each program reference the common (because the C library is common,) one instance of that library, instead of having each program contain a copy of the library.

This is implemented during the linking process where some of the objects are linked during the link time whereas some done during the run time (deferred/dynamic linking).

STATICALLY LINKING:

The term 'statically linked' means that the binding between the program and the particular library is fixed and known at link time before the program run. This binding can't be changed, unless we re-link the program with a new version of the library.

Programs that are linked statically are linked against archives of objects (libraries) that typically have the extension of .a. e.g. libc.a

The limitation of this technique is that the executable is quite big in size, all the needed information need to be brought together.

DYNAMICALLY LINKING:

The term 'dynamically linked' means that the binding between the program and the shared object is done at runtime that is before the program starts, the appropriate shared objects are found and bound.

The linker places information into the executable that tells the loader which shared object module the code is in and which runtime linker should be used to find and bind the references.

Programs that are linked dynamically are linked against shared objects that have the extension .so. e.g. libc.so

Advantages:

Program files (on disk) become much smaller because they need not hold all necessary text and data segments information. It is very useful for portability.

In combination with virtual memory, dynamic linking permits two or more processes to share read-only executable modules such as standard C libraries. Using this technique, only one copy of a module needs be resident in memory at any time, and multiple processes, each can executes this shared code (read only). This results in a considerable memory saving, although demands an efficient swapping policy.

2.3.2 LOADING

In Linux processes loaded from a file system (using either the execve() or spawn() system calls) are in ELF format. This elf format contains various sections such as .init,.text,.bss.got,.data,.ctors,.dtors as shown in above elf format(my_pattern.elf.txt)

When the .exe(executable) runs, before running this need to load into memory.

This is done by the loader, which is generally part of the operating system. The loader does the following things (from other things):

Memory and access validation - Firstly, the OS system kernel reads in the program file's header information and does the validation for type, access permissions, memory requirement and its ability to run its instructions. It confirms that file is an executable image and calculates memory requirements.

Process setup includes:

- Allocates primary memory for the program's execution.
- Copies address space from secondary to primary memory.
- Copies the .text and .data sections from the executable into primary memory.
- Copies program arguments (e.g., command line arguments) onto the stack.
- Initializes registers: sets the esp (stack pointer) to point to top of stack, clears the rest.
- Jumps to start routine, which: copies main ()'s arguments off of the stack, and jumps to main().

i.e. The operating system logically copies a file's segment to a virtual memory segment according to the information provided in the program header table. The OS can also use segments to create a shared memory resource.

Address space is memory space that contains program code, stack, and data segments or in other word, all data the program uses as it runs. The memory layout, consists of three segments (text, data, and stack).

3. Embedded Software Development Process

When build tools run on the same system as the program they produce, they can make a lot of assumptions about the system. This is typically not the case in embedded software development, where the build tools run on a host computer that differs from the target hardware platform. There are a lot of things that software development tools can do automatically when the target platform is well defined.

This automation is possible because the tools can exploit features of the hardware and operating system on which your program will execute. For example, if all of your programs will be executed on IBM-compatible PCs running Windows, your compiler can automate—and, therefore, hide from your view—certain aspects of the software build process.

Embedded software development tools, on the other hand, can rarely make assumptions about the target platform. Instead, the user must provide some of her own knowledge of the system to the tools by giving them more explicit instructions.

The process of converting the source code representation of your embedded software into an executable binary image involves three distinct steps:

- Each of the source files must be compiled or assembled into an object file.
- All of the object files that result from the first step must be linked together to produce a single object file, called the relocatable program.

- Physical memory addresses must be assigned to the relative offsets within the relocatable program in a process called relocation.

The result of the final step is a file containing an executable binary image that is ready to run on the embedded system.

The embedded software development process just described is illustrated in Figure below. In this figure, the three steps are shown from top to bottom, with the tools that perform the steps shown in boxes that have rounded corners.

Each of these development tools takes one or more files as input and produces a single output file. More specific information about these tools and the files they produce is provided in the sections that follow.

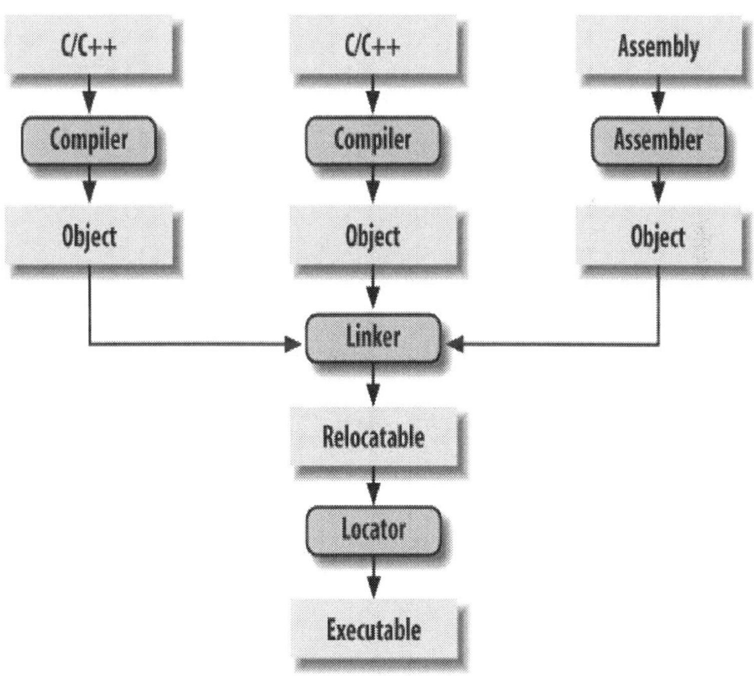

Figure 3.1 - Embedded SW Development Process

Each of the steps of the embedded software build process is a transformation performed by software running on a general-purpose computer. To distinguish this development computer (usually a PC or Unix workstation) from the target embedded system, it is referred to as the host computer.

The compiler, assembler, linker, and locator run on a host computer rather than on the embedded system itself. Yet, these tools combine their efforts to produce an executable binary image that will execute properly only on the target embedded system.

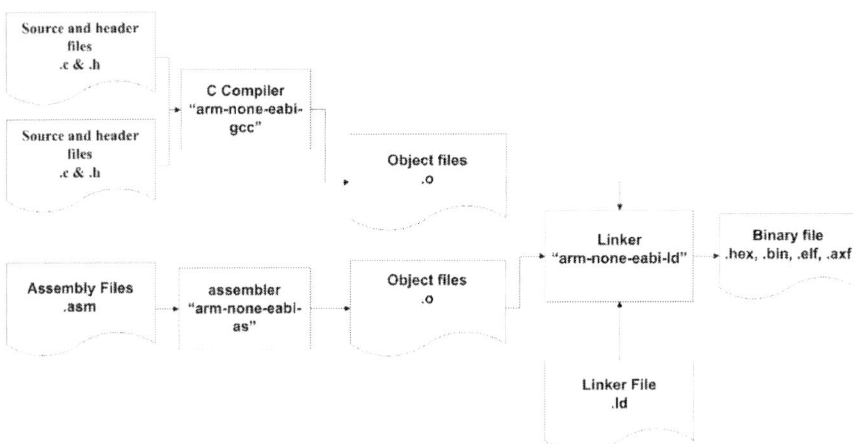

Figure 3.2 – Build Process of Embedded C Program.

4. SDLC - Verification and Validation Model

Verification and Validation (V&V) is the process of checking that a software system meets specifications and that it fulfils its intended purpose. It is normally part of the software testing process of a project.
According to the Capability Maturity Model (CMMI-SW v1.1),

- Verification: The process of evaluating software to determine whether the products of a given development phase satisfy the conditions imposed at the start of that phase.

- Validation: The process of evaluating software during or at the end of the development process to determine whether it satisfies specified requirements.

- **Verification** shows conformance with specification; **validation** shows that the program meets the customer's needs.

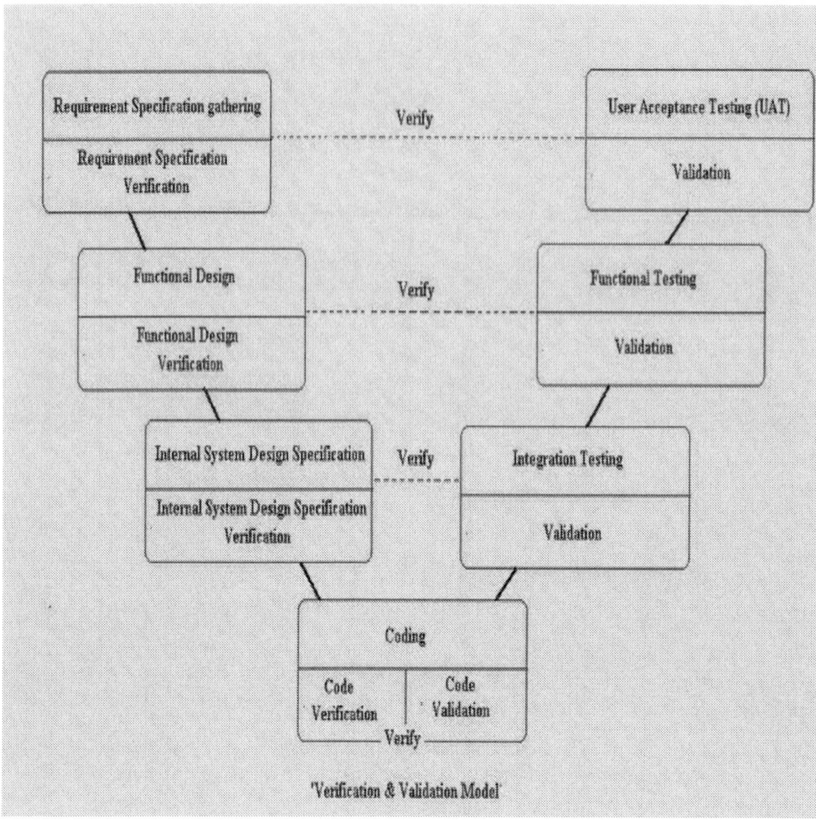

Figure 4.1 – V&V Model

The **V-model** represents a software development process (also applicable to hardware development) which may be considered an extension of the waterfall model. Instead of moving down in a linear way, the process steps are bent upwards after the coding phase, to form the typical V shape. The V-Model demonstrates the relationships between each phase of the development life cycle and its associated phase of testing.
The V model has a number of benefits:

- Systems development projects usually have a test approach, or test strategy document, which defines how testing will be performed throughout the lifecycle of the project. The V model provides a consistent basis and standard for part of that strategy.

- The V model explicitly suggests that testing (quality assurance) should be considered early on in the life of a project. Testing and fixing can be done at any stage in the lifecycle. However, the cost of finding and fixing faults increases dramatically as development progresses.

- Evidence suggests that if a fault uncovered during design costs 1.0 monetary unit to correct, then the same fault uncovered just before testing will cost 6.5 units, during testing 15 units, and after release between 60 and 100 units. The need to find faults as soon as possible reinforces the need for the quality assurance of documents such as the requirements specification and the functional specification. This is performed using static testing techniques such as inspections and walkthroughs.

- It introduces the idea of specifying test requirements and expected outcomes prior to performing the actual tests. For example, the acceptance tests are performed against a specification of requirements, rather than against some criteria dreamed up when the acceptance stage has been reached

- The V model provides a focus for defining the testing that must take place within each stage. The definition of testing is assisted by the idea of entry and exit criteria. Hence, the model can be used to define the state a deliverable must be in before it can enter and leave each stage.

- The exit criteria of one stage are usually the entry criteria of the next. In many organizations, there is concern about the quality of the program code released by individual programmers. Some programmers release code that appears to be fault-free, while others release code that still has many faults in it.

- The problem of programmers releasing code with different levels of robustness would be addressed in the exit criteria of unit design and unit testing. Unit design would require programmers to specify their intended test cases before they wrote any program code.

- Coding could not begin until these test cases had been agreed with an appropriate manager. Second, the test cases would have to be conducted successfully before the program could leave the unit test stage and be released to integration testing.

- Finally, the V model provides a basis for defining who is responsible for performing the testing at each stage. Here are some typical responsibilities:

    - acceptance testing performed by users
    - system testing performed by system testers
    - integration testing performed by program team leaders
    - Unit testing performed by programmers.

The V model is therefore an excellent basis for the partitioning of testing, highlighting the fact that all the participants in the development of a system have a responsibility for quality assurance and testing.

5. Storage Classes in C

There are 4 Storage Classes in C

1. AUTO
2. EXTERN
3. STATIC
4. REGISTER

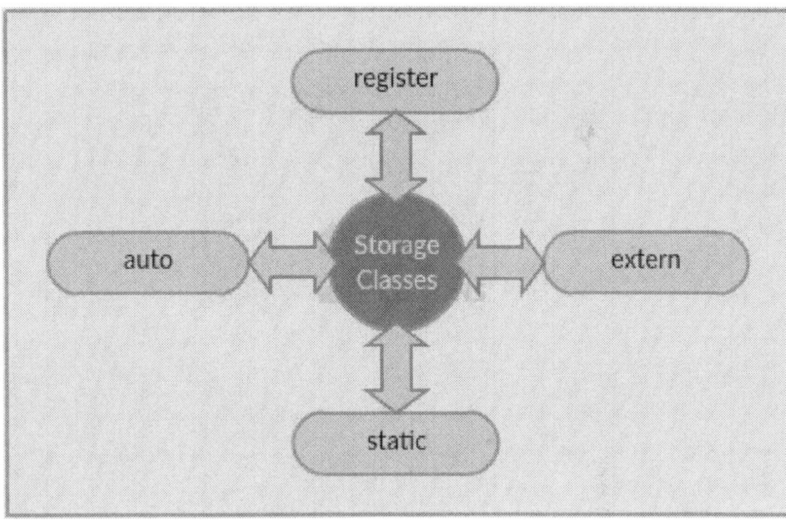

Storage Specifier	Storage	Initial value	Scope	Life
auto	Stack	Garbage	Within block	End of block
extern	Data segment	Zero	global Multiple files	Till end of program
static	Data segment	Zero	Within block	Till end of program
register	CPU Register	Garbage	Within block	End of block

Figure 5.1 – Storage Classes in C

Auto storage class

A variable declared inside a function without any storage class specification, is by default an automatic variable. They are created when a function is called and are destroyed automatically when the function exits. Automatic variables can also be called local variables because they are local to a function. By default, they are assigned garbage value by the compiler.

```
void main()
{
int detail;
or
auto int detail;   //Both are same
}
```

External or Global storage class

A variable that is declared outside any function is a Global variable. Global variables remain available throughout the entire program. One important thing to remember about global variable is that their values can be changed by any function in the program.

```
int number;
void main()
{
number =10;
}
fun1()
{
number =20;
}
fun2()
```

```
{
number =30;
}
```

Here the global variable number is available to all three functions.

Extern keyword

The extern keyword is used before a variable to inform the compiler that this variable is declared somewhere else. The extern declaration does not allocate storage for variables.

Static storage class

A static variable tells the compiler to persist the variable until the end of program. Instead of creating and destroying a variable every time when it comes into and goes out of scope, static is initialized only once and remains into existence till the end of program.

A static variable can either be internal or external depending upon the place of declaration. Scope of internal static variable remains inside the function in which it is defined. External static variables remain restricted to scope of file in each they are declared.

They are assigned 0 (zero) as default value by the compiler.

```
void test();

main()
{
```

```
test();
test();
test();
}
void test()
{
static int a = 0;       //Static variable
a = a+1;
printf("%d\t",a);
}
output :
1   2       3
```

Register storage class

Register variable inform the compiler to store the variable in register instead of memory. Register variable has faster access than normal variable. Frequently used variables are kept in register. Only few variables can be placed inside register. We can never get the address of such variables.

```
register int number;
```

6. Interrupts

Interrupts (also known as traps or exceptions in some processors) are a technique of diverting the processor from the execution of the current program so that it may deal with some event that has occurred.

Such an event may be an error from a peripheral, or simply that an I/O device has finished the last task it was given and is now ready for another. An interrupt is generated in your computer every time you type a key or move the mouse. You can think of it as a hardware-generated function call.

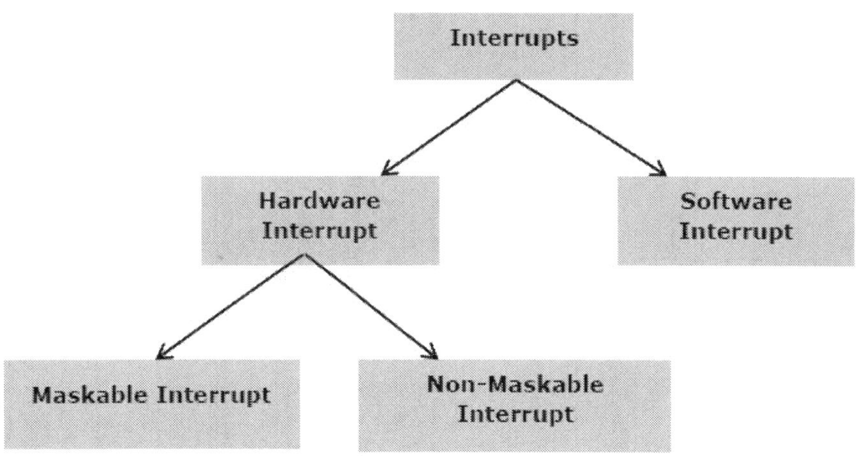

Figure 6.1 - Interrupts

Hardware Interrupts

There are two ways of telling when an I/O device (such as a serial controller or a disk controller) is ready for the next sequence of data to be transferred. The first is busy waiting or polling, where the processor continuously checks the device's status register until the device is ready. This wastes the processor's time but is the simplest to implement. For some time-critical applications, polling can reduce the time it takes for the processor to respond to a change of state in a peripheral.

Software Interrupts

A software interrupt is generated by an instruction. It is the lowest-priority interrupt and is generally used by programs to request a service to be performed by the system software (operating system or firmware).

Difference b/w Hardware Interrupt and Software Interrupt

An interrupt is a special signal that causes the computer's central processing unit to suspend what it is doing and transfers its control to a special program called an **interrupt handler**. The responsibility of an interrupt handler is to determine what caused the interrupt, service the interrupt and then return the control to the point from where the interrupt was caused. The difference between **hardware interrupt** and **software interrupt** is as below:

Hardware Interrupt: This interrupt is caused by some external device such as request to start an I/O or occurrence of a hardware failure.

Software Interrupt: This interrupt can be invoked with the help of INT instruction. A programmer triggered this event that immediately stops execution of the program and passes execution over to the INT handler. The INT handler is usually a part of the operating system

and determines the action to be taken e.g. output to the screen, execute file etc.
Thus a software interrupt as it's name suggests is driven by a software instruction and a hardware interrupt is the result of external causes.

Interrupt latency

Interrupt latency is the time between interrupt request and execution of first instruction of the ISR.

We need a oscilloscope or a logic state analyzer. By entering the interrupt service routine (ISR), you need to activate an available port on your hardware (like a led port or so on) and deactivate it just before returning from the ISR. You can do that by writing the appropriate code.

By connecting one input of the oscilloscope (or logic state analyzer) to the INTR pin of the microprocessor and the second one to the port you activate/deactivate, you can measure the latency time and the duration of the ISR

Causes of interrupt latencies:

- The first delay is typically in the hardware: The interrupt request signal needs to be synchronized to the CPU clock. Depending on the synchronization logic, typically up to 3 CPU cycles can be lost before the interrupt request has reached the CPU core.

- The CPU will typically complete the current instruction. This instruction can take a lot of cycles; on most systems, divide, push-multiple or memory-copy instructions are the instructions which require most clock cycles.

- On top of the cycles required by the CPU, there are in most cases additional cycles required for memory access. In an ARM7 system, the instruction STMDB SP!,{R0-R11,LR}; Push parameters and perm. Registers is typically the worst case instruction. It stores 13 32-bit registers on the stack. The CPU requires 15 clock cycles. The memory system may require additional cycles for wait states.
- After completion of the current instruction, the CPU performs a mode switch or pushes registers (typically PC and flag registers) on the stack. In general, modern CPUs (such as ARM) perform a mode switch, which requires less CPU cycles than saving registers.

- Pipeline fill: Most modern CPUs are pipelined. Execution of an instruction happens in various stages of the pipeline. An instruction is executed when it has reached its final stage of the pipeline. Since the mode switch has flushed the pipeline, a few extra cycles are required to refill the pipeline.

7. RTOS & SW Architecture

Real-Time Operating System is a multitasking operating system intended for real-time applications. It is used on every device/system needing real time operations that means operations based not only on correctness but also upon the time (clock cycles) in which they are performed.

In general, an operating system (OS) is responsible for managing the hardware resources of a computer and hosting applications that run on the computer. An RTOS performs these tasks, but is also specially designed to run applications with very precise timing and a high degree of reliability.

This can be especially important in measurement and automation systems where downtime is costly or a program delay could cause a safety hazard. To be considered "real-time", an operating system must have a known maximum time for each of the critical operations that it performs (or at least be able to guarantee that maximum most of the time). Some of these operations include OS calls and interrupt handling.

Operating systems that can absolutely guarantee a maximum time for these operations are commonly referred to as "hard real-time", while operating systems that can only guarantee a maximum most of the time are referred to as "soft real-time".

Example: Imagine that you are designing an airbag system for a new model of car. In this case, a small error in timing (causing the airbag to deploy too early or too late) could be catastrophic and cause injury.

Therefore, a hard-real-time system is needed; you need assurance as the system designer that no single operation will exceed certain timing constraints. On the other hand, if you were to design a mobile phone that received streaming video, it may be ok to lose a small amount of data occasionally even though on average it is important to keep up with the video stream. For this application, a soft real-time operating system may suffice.

An RTOS can guarantee that a program will run with very consistent timing. Real-time operating systems do this by providing programmers with a high degree of control over how tasks are prioritized, and typically also allow checking to make sure that important deadlines are met.

How RTOS Differ from General-Purpose OSs?

Operating systems such as Microsoft Windows and Mac OS can provide an excellent platform for developing and running your non-critical measurement and control applications. However, these operating systems are designed for different use cases than real-time operating systems, and are not the ideal platform for running applications that require precise timing or extended up-time.

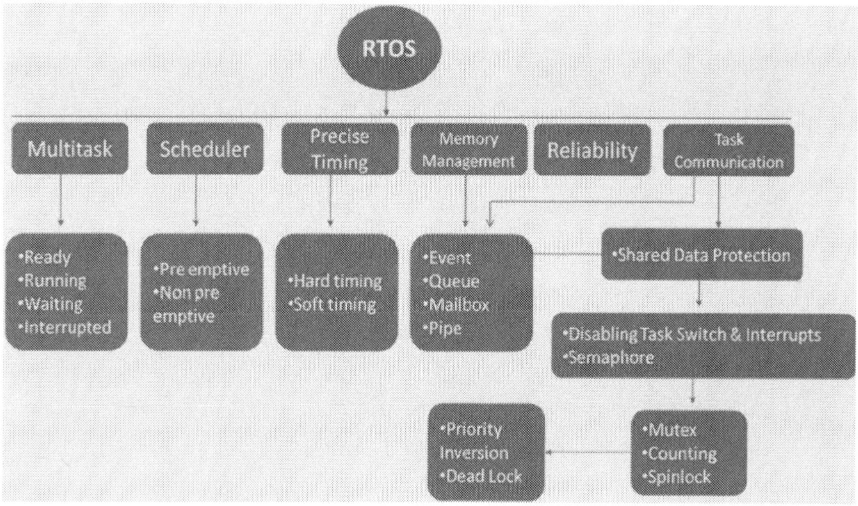

Figure 7.1 RTOS

Software Architecture:

Vonneuman and Harvard architecture

The name Harvard Architecture comes from the Harvard Mark I relay-based computer. The most obvious characteristic of the Harvard Architecture is that it has physically separate signals and storage for code and data memory.

It is possible to access program memory and data memory simultaneously. Typically, code (or program) memory is read-only and data memory is read-write. Therefore, it is impossible for program contents to be modified by the program itself.

The Von-Neumann Architecture is named after the mathematician and early computer scientist John von Neumann. Von Neumann machines have shared signals and memory for code and data. Thus, the program can be easily modified by itself since it is stored in read-write memory.

Harvard architecture has separate data and instruction busses, allowing transfers to be performed simultaneously on both buses. **Von Neumann architecture** has only one bus which is used for both data transfers and instruction fetches, and therefore data transfers and instruction fetches must be scheduled – they cannot be performed at the same time.

It is possible to have two separate memory systems for a **Harvard architecture**. As long as data and instructions can be fed in at the same time, then it doesn't matter whether it comes from a cache or memory. But there are problems with this.

Compilers generally embed data (literal pools) within the code, and it is often also necessary to be able to write to the instruction memory space, for example in the case of self-modifying code, or, if an ARM debugger is used, to set software breakpoints in memory. If there are two completely separate, isolated memory systems, this is not possible. There must be some kind of bridge between the memory systems to allow this.

Using a simple, unified memory system together with a Harvard architecture is highly inefficient. Unless it is possible to feed data into both buses at the same time, it might be better to use a von Neumann architecture processor.

Use of caches:

At higher clock speeds, caches are useful as the memory speed is proportionally slower. **Harvard architectures** tend to be targeted at higher performance systems, and so caches are nearly always used in such systems.

Von Neumann architectures usually have a single unified cache, which stores both instructions and data. The proportion of each in the cache is variable, which may be a good thing. It would in principle be possible to have separate instruction and data caches, storing data and instructions separately. This probably would not be very useful as it would only be possible to ever access one cache at a time.

Caches for Harvard architectures are very useful. Such a system would have separate caches for each bus. Trying to use a shared cache on a Harvard architecture would be very inefficient since then only one bus can be fed at a time. Having two caches means it is possible to feed both buses simultaneously exactly what is necessary for a Harvard architecture.

This also allows to have a very simple unified memory system, using the same address space for both instructions and data. This gets around the problem of literal pools and self-modifying code. What it does mean, however, is that when starting with empty caches, it is necessary to fetch instructions and data from the single memory system, at the same time. Obviously, two memory accesses are needed therefore before the core has all the data needed.

This performance will be no better than a von Neumann architecture. However, as the caches fill up, it is much more likely that the instruction or data value has already been cached, and so only one of the two has to be fetched from memory. The other can be supplied directly from the cache with no additional delay. The best performance is achieved when both instructions and data are supplied by the caches, with no need to access external memory at all.

This is the most sensible compromise and the architecture used by ARMs Harvard processor cores. Two separate memory systems can perform better, but would be difficult to implement.

8. Concepts in C

8.1 What is the difference between declaration and definition?

Definition means where a variable or function is defined in reality and actual memory is allocated for variable or function.

Declaration means just giving a reference of a variable and function.

8.2 RISC and CISC differences?

CISC: (Complex **I**nstruction **S**et **C**omputer)
Eg: Intel and AMD CPU's

- CISC chips have a large amount of different and complex instructions.
- CISC chips are relatively slow (compared to RISC chips) per instruction, but use little (less than RISC) instructions.
- CISC architecture is to complete a task in as few lines of assembly as possible. This is achieved by building processor hardware that is capable of understanding and executing a series of operations.
- In CISC, compiler has to do very little work to translate a high-level language statement into assembly. Because the length of the code is relatively short, very little RAM is required to store instructions. The emphasis is put on building complex instructions directly into the hardware.
- When executed, this instruction loads the two values into separate registers, multiplies the operands in the execution unit, and then stores the product in the appropriate register.

RISC: (Reduced **I**nstruction **S**et **C**omputer**)**
Eg: Apple, ARM processors

- Fewer, simpler and faster instructions would be better, than the large, complex and slower CISC instructions. However, more instructions are needed to accomplish a task.
- RISC chips require fewer transistors, which makes them easier to design and cheaper to produce.
- it's easier to write powerful optimized compilers, since fewer instructions exist.
- RISC is cheaper and faster.
- RISC puts a greater burden on the software. Software needs to become more complex. Software developers need to write more lines for the same tasks. Therefore they argue that RISC is not the architecture of the future, since conventional CISC chips are becoming faster and cheaper
- Simple instructions that can be executed within one clock cycle.
- "MULT" command described above could be divided into three separate commands: "LOAD," which moves data from the memory bank to a register, "PROD," which finds the product of two operands located within the registers, and "STORE," which moves data from a register to the memory banks.
- At first, this may seem like a much less efficient way of completing the operation. Because there are more lines of code, more RAM is needed to store the assembly level instructions. The compiler must also perform more work to convert a high-level language statement into code of this form.
- Separating the "LOAD" and "STORE" instructions actually reduces the amount of work that the computer must perform.
- Major problem of RISC – they don't afford the widespread compatibility, that x86 chips do.

8.3 What are the startup code steps?

1. Disable all the interrupts.
2. Copy and initialized data from ROM to RAM.

3. Zero the uninitialized data area.
4. Allocate space and for initialize the stack.
5. Initialize the processor stack pointer
6. Call main

8.4 What are the booting steps for a CPU?

- The power supply does a self-check and sends a power-good signal to the CPU.
  The CPU starts executing the code stored in ROM on the motherboard starts the address 0xFFFF0.

- The routines in ROM test the central hardware, search for video ROM, perform a checksum on the video ROM and executes the routines in video ROM.
- The routines in the mother board ROM then continue searching for any ROM, checksum and executes these routines.
- After performing the POST (Power On-Self Test) is executed. The system will search for a boot device.
- Assuming that the valid boot device is found, IO.SYS is loaded into memory and executed.IO.SYS consists primarily of initialization code and extension to the memory board ROM BIOS.
- MSDOS.SYS is loaded into memory and executed. MSDOS.SYS contains the DOS routines.
- CONFIG.SYS (created and modified by the user. load additional device drivers for peripheral devices), COMMAND.COM (It is command interpreter- It translates the commands entered by the user. It also contains internal DOS commands.
- It executes and AUTOEXEC.BAT),AUTOEXEC.BAT (It contains all the commands that the user wants which are executed automatically every time the computed is started).

8.5 What Little-Endian and Big-Endian?

First of all, Do you know what Little-Endian and Big-Endian mean? Little Endian means that the lower order byte of the number is stored in memory at the lowest address, and the higher order byte is stored at the highest address. That is, the little end comes first.
For example, a 4 byte, 32-bit integerByte3 Byte2 Byte1 Byte0will be arranged in memory as follows:
Base_Address+0 Byte0
Base_Address+1 Byte1
Base_Address+2 Byte2
Base_Address+3 Byte3

Intel processors use "Little Endian" byte order.
"Big Endian" means that the higher order byte of the number is stored in memory at the lowest address, and the lower order byte at the highest address. The big end comes first.
Base_Address+0 Byte3
Base_Address+1 Byte2
Base_Address+2 Byte1
Base_Address+3 Byte0

Motorola, Solaris processors use "Big Endian" byte order.In "Little Endian" form, code which picks up a 1, 2, 4, or longer byte number proceed in the same way for all formats. They first pick up the lowest order byte at offset 0 and proceed from there. Also, because of the 1:1 relationship between address offset and byte number (offset 0 is byte 0), multiple precision mathematic routines are easy to code. In "Big Endian" form, since the high-order byte comes first, the code can test whether the number is positive or negative by looking at the byte at offset zero.

Its not required to know how long the number is, nor does the code have to skip over any bytes to find the byte containing the sign information. The numbers are also stored in the order in which they are printed out, so binary to decimal routines are particularly efficient. Here is some code to determine what the type of your machine is.

```
int num = 1;
if(*(char *)&num == 1)
{
printf("\nLittle-Endian\n");
}
else
{
printf("Big-Endian\n");
}And here is some code to convert from one Endian
to another.int myreversefunc(int num)
{
int byte0, byte1, byte2, byte3;byte0 = (num & x000000FF) >> 0 ;
byte1 = (num & x0000FF00) >> 8 ;
byte2 = (num & x00FF0000) >> 16 ;
byte3 = (num & xFF000000) >> 24 ;return((byte0 << 24) | (byte1
<< 16) | (byte2 << 8) | (byte3 << 0));
}
```

8.6 Constant and Volatile Variables

Can a variable be both *const* and *volatile*?

Yes. The const modifier means that this code cannot change the value of the variable, but that does not mean that the value cannot be changed by means outside this code.
The timer structure was accessed through a volatile const pointer. The function itself did not change the value of the timer, so it was declared const. However, the value was changed by hardware on the computer, so it was declared volatile. If a variable is both const and volatile, the two modifiers can appear in either order.

What are Constant and Volatile Qualifiers?

Const

const is used with a datatype declaration or definition to specify an unchanging value

Examples:

```
const int five = 5;
const double pi = 3.141593;
const objects may not be changed
The following are illegal:
const int five = 5;
const double pi = 3.141593;
pi = 3.2;
five = 6;
```

Volatile

Volatile specifies a variable whose value may be changed by processes outside the current program. One example of a volatile object might be a buffer used to exchange data with an external device:

```
int check_iobuf(void)
{
        volatile int iobuf;
        int val;

        while (iobuf == 0) {
        }
        val = iobuf;
        iobuf = 0;
        return(val);
```

```
}
```

If iobuf had not been declared volatile, the compiler would notice that nothing happens inside the loop and thus eliminate the loop const and volatile can be used together

An input-only buffer for an external device could be declared as const volatile (or volatile const, order is not important) to make sure the compiler knows that the variable should not be changed (because it is input-only) and that its value may be altered by processes other than the current program

The keywords const and volatile can be applied to any declaration, including those of structures, unions, enumerated types or typedef names. Applying them to a declaration is called qualifying the declaration—that's why const and volatile are called type qualifiers, rather than type specifiers. Here are a few representative examples:

```
volatile i;
volatile int j;
const long q;
const volatile unsigned long int rt_clk;
struct{
      const long int li;
      signed char sc;
}volatile vs;
```

Don't be put off; some of them are deliberately complicated: what they mean will be explained later. Remember that they could also be further complicated by introducing storage class specifications as well! In fact, the truly spectacular

```
extern const volatile unsigned long int rt_clk;
```

is a strong possibility in some real-time operating system kernels.

Const

Let's look at what is meant when const is used. It's really quite simple: const means that something is not modifiable, so a data object that is declared with const as a part of its type specification must not be assigned to in any way during the run of a program.

It is very likely that the definition of the object will contain an initializer (otherwise, since you can't assign to it, how would it ever get a value?), but this is not always the case. For example, if you were accessing a hardware port at a fixed memory address and promised only to read from it, then it would be declared to be const but not initialized.

Taking the address of a data object of a type which isn't const and putting it into a pointer to the const-qualified version of the same type is both safe and explicitly permitted; you will be able to use the pointer to inspect the object, but not modify it.

Putting the address of a const type into a pointer to the unqualified type is much more dangerous and consequently prohibited (although you can get around this by using a cast).

```
#include <stdio.h>
#include <stdlib.h>

main(){
      int i;
      const int ci = 123;

      /* declare a pointer to a const.. */
      const int *cpi;

      /* ordinary pointer to a non-const */
      int *ncpi;
```

```
    cpi = &ci;
    ncpi = &i;

    /*
     * this is allowed
     */
    cpi = ncpi;

    /*
     * this needs a cast
     * because it is usually a big mistake,
     * see what it permits below.
     */
    ncpi = (int *)cpi;

    /*
     * now to get undefined behaviour...
     * modify a const through a pointer
     */
    *ncpi = 0;

    exit(EXIT_SUCCESS);
}
```

As the example shows, it is possible to take the address of a constant object, generate a pointer to a non-constant, then use the new pointer. This is an *error* in your program and results in undefined behaviour.

The main intention of introducing const objects was to allow them to be put into read-only store, and to permit compilers to do extra consistency checking in a program.

Unless you defeat the intent by doing naughty things with pointers, a compiler is able to check that const objects are not modified explicitly by the user.
An interesting extra feature pops up now. What does this mean?

```
char c;

char *const cp = &c;
```

It's simple really cp is a pointer to a char, which is exactly what it would be if the const weren't there. The const means that cp is not to be modified, although whatever it points to can be the pointer is constant, not the thing that it points to. The other way round is

```
const char *cp;
```

Which means that now cp is an ordinary, modifiable pointer, but the thing that it points to must not be modified. So, depending on what you choose to do, both the pointer and the thing it points to may be modifiable or not; just choose the appropriate declaration.

Volatile

After const, we treat volatile. The reason for having this type qualifier is mainly to do with the problems that are encountered in real-time or embedded systems programming using C. Imagine that you are writing code that controls a hardware device by placing appropriate values in hardware registers at known absolute addresses.
Let's imagine that the device has two registers, each 16 bits long, at ascending memory addresses; the first one is the control and status register (csr) and the second is a data port. The traditional way of accessing such a device is like this:

```
/* Standard C example but without const or volatile */

/*

* Declare the device registers

* Whether to use int or short

* is implementation dependent

*/

struct devregs{

       unsigned short  csr;    /* control & status */

       unsigned short  data;   /* data port */

};

/* bit patterns in the csr */

#define ERROR   0x1

#define READY   0x2

#define RESET   0x4

/* absolute address of the device */

#define DEVADDR ((struct devregs *)0xffff0004)
```

```
/* number of such devices in system */

#define NDEVS   4

/*

* Busy-wait function to read a byte from device n.

* check range of device number.

* Wait until READY or ERROR

* if no error, read byte, return it

* otherwise reset error, return 0xffff

*/

unsigned int read_dev(unsigned devno){

      struct devregs *dvp = DEVADDR + devno;

      if(devno >= NDEVS)

            return(0xffff);

      while((dvp->csr & (READY | ERROR)) == 0)

            ; /* NULL - wait till done */

      if(dvp->csr & ERROR){
```

```
        dvp->csr = RESET;

        return(0xffff);

    }

    return((dvp->data) & 0xff);

}
```

The technique of using a structure declaration to describe the device register layout and names is very common practice. Notice that there aren't actually any objects of that type defined, so the declaration simply indicates the structure without using up any store.

To access the device registers, an appropriately cast constant is used as if it were pointing to such a structure, but of course it points to memory addresses instead.

However, a major problem with previous C compilers would be in the while loop which tests the status register and waits for the ERROR or READY bit to come on.

Any self-respecting optimizing compiler would notice that the loop tests the same memory address over and over again. It would almost certainly arrange to reference memory once only, and copy the value into a hardware register, thus speeding up the loop.

This is, of course, exactly what we don't want; this is one of the few places where we must look at the place where the pointer points, every time around the loop.

Because of this problem, most C compilers have been unable to make that sort of optimization in the past. To remove the problem (and other similar ones to do with when to write to where a pointer points), the keyword volatile was introduced. It tells the compiler that the object is subject to sudden change for reasons which cannot be predicted from a study of the program itself, and forces every reference to such an object to be a genuine reference.

Here is how you would rewrite the example, making use of const and volatile to get what you want.

```
/*
* Declare the device registers
* Whether to use int or short
* is implementation dependent
*/

struct devregs{
      unsigned short volatile csr;
      unsigned short const volatile data;
};

/* bit patterns in the csr */
#define ERROR   0x1
#define READY   0x2
#define RESET   0x4

/* absolute address of the device */
#define DEVADDR ((struct devregs *)0xffff0004)

/* number of such devices in system */
#define NDEVS   4

/*
* Busy-wait function to read a byte from device n.
* check range of device number.
```

```
* Wait until READY or ERROR
* if no error, read byte, return it
* otherwise reset error, return 0xffff
*/
unsigned int read_dev(unsigned devno){

      struct devregs * const dvp = DEVADDR + devno;

      if(devno >= NDEVS)
            return(0xffff);

      while((dvp->csr & (READY | ERROR)) == 0)
            ; /* NULL - wait till done */

      if(dvp->csr & ERROR){
            dvp->csr = RESET;
            return(0xffff);
      }

      return((dvp->data) & 0xff);
}
```

The rules about mixing volatile and regular types resemble those for const. A pointer to a volatile object can be assigned the address of a regular object with safety, but it is dangerous (and needs a cast) to take the address of a volatile object and put it into a pointer to a regular object. Using such a derived pointer results in undefined behaviour.

If an array, union or structure is declared with const or volatile attributes, then all of the members take on that attribute too.

This makes sense when you think about it—how could a member of a const structure be modifiable?

That means that an alternative rewrite of the last example would be possible. Instead of declaring the device registers to be volatile in the structure, the pointer could have been declared to point to a volatile structure instead, like this:

```
struct devregs{
    unsigned short  csr;    /* control & status */
    unsigned short  data;   /* data port */
};
volatile struct devregs *const dvp=DEVADDR+devno;
```

Since dvp points to a volatile object, it not permitted to optimize references through the pointer. Our feeling is that, although this would work, it is bad style. The volatile declaration belongs in the structure: it is the device registers which are volatile and that is where the information should be kept; it reinforces the fact for a human reader.

So, for any object likely to be subject to modification either by hardware or asynchronous interrupt service routines, the volatile type qualifier is important.

Now, just when you thought that you understood all that, here comes the final twist. A declaration like this:

```
volatile struct devregs{

    /* stuff */

}v_decl;
```

declares the type struct devregs and also a volatile-qualified object of that type, called v_decl. A later declaration like this

```
struct devregs nv_decl;
```

declares nv_decl which is *not* qualified with volatile! The qualification is *not* part of the type of struct devregs but applies only to the declaration of v_decl. Look at it this way round, which perhaps makes the situation more clear (the two declarations are the same in their effect):

```
struct devregs{
    /* stuff */
}volatile v_decl;
```

If you do want to get a shorthand way of attaching a qualifier to another type, you can use typedef to do it:

```
struct x{
    int a;
};
typedef const struct x csx;

csx const_sx;
struct x non_const_sx = {1};

const_sx = non_const_sx;      /* error - attempt to modify a const */
```

8.7 What are the differences between a union and a structure in C?

A union is a way of providing an alternate way of describing the same memory area. In this way, you could have a struct that contains a union, so that the "static", or similar portion of the data is described first, and the portion that changes is described by the union. The idea of a union could be handled in a different way by having 2 different structs defined, and making a pointer to each kind of struct.

The pointer to struct "a" could be assigned to the value of a buffer, and the pointer to struct "b" could be assigned to the same buffer, but now a->some field and b->some otherfield are both located in the same buffer. That is the idea behind a union.

It gives different ways to break down the same buffer area. The difference between structure and union are:

1. union allocates the memory equal to the maximum memory required by the member of the union but structure allocates the memory equal to the total memory required by the members.

2. In union, one block is used by all the member of the union but in case of structure, each member has their own memory space

Difference Between Stucture and Union:

i. Access Members

We can access all the members of structure at anytime.

Only one member of union can be accessed at anytime.

ii. Memory Allocation

Memory is allocated for all variables.

Allocates memory for variable which variable require more memory.

iii. Initialization

All members of structure can be initialized Only the first member of a union can be initialized.

iv. Keyword

'struct' keyword is used to declare structure.

'union' keyword is used to declare union.

vi. Example:

```
struct item_mst
{
   int rno;
   char nm[50];
}it;

union item_mst
{
   int rno;
   char nm[50];
}it;
```

Difference in their Usage:

While structure enables us treat a number of different variables stored at different in memory a union enables us to treat the same space in memory as a number of different variables. That is a Union offers a way for a section of memory to be treated as a variable of one type on one occasion and as a different variable of a different type on another occasion.

There is frequent requirement while interacting with hardware to access access a byte or group of bytes simultaneously and sometimes each byte individually. Usually union is the answer.

Lets say a structure containing an int,char and float is created and a union containing int char float are declared.

struct TT{ int a; float b; char c; } Union UU{ int a; float b; char c; }
sizeof TT(struct) would be >9 bytes (compiler dependent-if int,float, char are taken as 4,4,1)
sizeof UU(Union) would be 4 bytes as supposed from above.If a variable in double exists in union then the size of union and struct would be 8 bytes and cumulative size of all variables in struct.

Detailed Example:

```
struct foo
{
char c;
long l;
char *p;
};

union bar
{
char c;
long l;
char *p;
};
```

A struct foo contains all of the elements c, l, and p. Each element is separate and distinct.

A union bar contains only one of the elements c, l, and p at any given time.

Each element is stored in the same memory location (well, they all start at the same memory location), and you can only refer to the element which was last stored. (ie: after "barptr->c = 2;" you cannot reference
any of the other elements, such as "barptr->p" without invoking undefined behavior.)

Try the following program. (Yes, I know it invokes the above-mentioned "undefined behavior", but most likely will give some sort of output on most computers.)

```
struct foo
{
char c;
long l;
char *p;
};

union bar
{
char c;
long l;
char *p;
};

int main(int argc,char *argv[])
{
struct foo myfoo;
union bar mybar;

myfoo.c = 1;
myfoo.l = 2L;
```

```
myfoo.p = "This is myfoo";

mybar.c = 1;
mybar.l = 2L;
mybar.p = "This is mybar";

printf("myfoo: %d %ld %s\n",myfoo.c,myfoo.l,myfoo.p);
printf("mybar: %d %ld %s\n",mybar.c,mybar.l,mybar.p);

return 0;
}

On my system, I get:

myfoo: 1 2 This is myfoo
mybar: 100 4197476 This is mybar
```

Structure: Structure is a combination elements, which can be predefined data types or other structure. The length/size of the structure is the sum of the length of its elements.
In C, structures cannot contain functions. in C++ it can.

Union: Union is a combination elements, which can be predefined data types or other union. But, the size/length of union is the maximum of internal elements the *sizeof()* operator returns the size slightly more than calculated size due to padding, which again depends on OS.

Union allocates the memory equal to the maximum memory required by the member of the union but structure allocates the memory equal to the total memory required by the members. In union one block is used by all the member of the union but in case of structure, each member have their own memory space.

8.8 What is meant by structure padding?

Compilers pad structures to optimize data transfers. This is an hardware architecture issue. Most modern CPUs perform best when fundamental types, like 'int' or 'float', are aligned on memory boundaries of a particular size (eg. often a 4byte word on 32bit archs).

Many architectures don't allow misaligned access or if they do inoccur a performance penality.
When a compiler processes a structure declaration it will add extra bytes between fields to meet alignment needs.Most processors require specific memory alignment on variables certain types. Normally the minimum alignment is the size of the basic type in question, for instance this is common
char variables can be byte aligned and appear at any byte boundary
short (2 byte) variables must be 2 byte aligned, they can appear at any even byte boundary. This means that 0x10004567 is not a valid location for a short variable but 0x10004566 is.

long (4 byte) variables must be 4 byte aligned, they can only appear at byte boundaries that are a multiple of 4 bytes. This means that 0x10004566 is not a valid location for a long variable but 0x10004568 is.

Structure padding occurs because the members of the structure must appear at the correct byte boundary, to achieve this the compiler puts in padding bytes (or bits if bit fields are in use) so that the structure members appear in the correct location. Additionally the size of the structure must be such that in an array of the structures all the structures are correctly aligned in memory so there may be padding bytes at the end of the structure too

```
struct example {
char c1;
short s1;
char c2;
long l1;
char c3;
}
```

In this structure, assuming the alignment scheme I have previously stated then

c1 can appear at any byte boundary, however s1 must appear at a 2 byte boundary so there is a padding byte between c1 and s1.

c2 can then appear in the available memory location, however l1 must be at a 4 byte boundary so there are 3 padding bytes between c2 and l1

c3 then appear in the available memory location, however because the structure contains a long member the structure must be 4 byte aligned and must be a multiple of 4 bytes in size. Therefore there are 3 padding bytes at the end of the structure. It would appear in memory in this order

c1
padding byte
s1 byte 1
s1 byte 2
c2
padding byte
padding byte
padding byte
l1 byte 1
l1 byte 2
l1 byte 3

l1 byte 4
c3
padding byte
padding byte
padding byte

The structure would be 16 bytes long.

re-written like this

```
struct example {
long l1;
short s1;
char c1;
char c2;
char c3;
}
```

Then l1 appears at the correct byte alignment, s1 will be correctly aligned so no need for padding between l1 and s1. c1, c2, c3 can appear at any location. The structure must be a multiple of 4 bytes in size since it contains a long so 3 padding bytes appear after c3
It appears in memory in the order

l1 byte 1
l1 byte 2
l1 byte 3
l1 byte 4
s1 byte 1
s1 byte 2
c1
c2
c3
padding byte

padding byte
padding byte

and is only 12 bytes long.

I should point out that structure packing is platform and compiler (and in some cases compiler switch) dependent.

Memory Pools are just a section of memory reserved for allocating temporarily to other parts of the application

A memory leak occurs when you allocate some memory from the heap (or a pool) and then delete all references to that memory without returning it to the pool it was allocated from.

Program:

```
struct  MyStructA {
  char a;
  char b;
  int   c;
};

struct MyStructB {
  char a;
  int   c;
  char b;
};

int main(void) {
      int sizeA = sizeof(struct MyStructA);
      int sizeB = sizeof(struct MyStructB);

      printf("A = %d\n", sizeA);
      printf("B = %d\n", sizeB);
```

```
    return 0;
}
```

8.9 Difference between re-entrant function and recursive function in C

Re entrant function is a function which guaranteed that which can be work well under multi threaded environment. mean while function is access by one thread, another thread can call it mean there is separate execution stack and handling for each. So function should not contain any static or shared variable which can harm or disturb the execution. Mean function which can be called by thread, while running from another thread safely and properly

Example:

```
int t;

void swap(int *x, int *y)
{
 int s;

 s = t; // save global variable
 t = *x;
 *x = *y;
 // hardware interrupt might invoke isr() here!
 *y = t;
 t = s; // restore global variable
}

void isr()
{
 int x = 1, y = 2;
 swap(&x, &y);
```

```
}
```

Recursive function Example:

```
void doll ( int size )
{
if ( size == 0 )   // No doll can be smaller than 1 atom (10^0==1) so
doesn't call itself
return;          // Return does not have to return something, it can
be used
//  to exit a function
doll ( size – 1 ); // Decrements the size variable so the next doll
will be smaller.
}
int main()
{
doll ( 10 ); //Starts off with a large doll (it's a logarithmic scale)
```

8.10 What is Watchdog timer?

A watchdog timer (or computer operating properly (COP) timer) is a computer hardware or software timer that triggers a system reset or other corrective action if the main program, due to some fault condition, such as a hang, neglects to regularly service the watchdog (writing a "service pulse" to it, also referred to as "kicking the dog", "petting the dog", "feeding the watchdog" or "waking the watchdog"). The intention is to bring the system back from the unresponsive state into normal operation. Watchdog timers can be more complex, attempting to save debug information onto a persistent medium; i.e. information useful for debugging the problem that caused the fault. In this case a second, simpler, watchdog timer ensures that if the first watchdog timer does not report completion of its information saving task within a certain amount of time, the system will reset with or without the information saved. The most common use of watchdog timers is in embedded systems, where this specialized timer is often a built-in unit of a microcontroller.

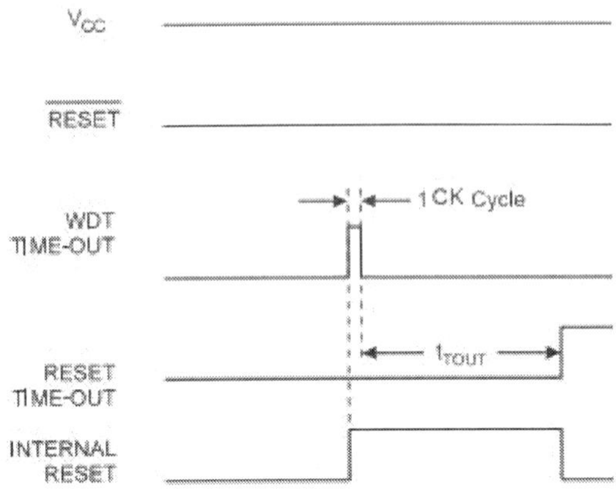

8.11 What is a Function Pointer ?

A function pointer is a variable that stores the address of a function that can later be called through that function pointer. This is useful because functions encapsulate behavior. For instance, every time you need a particular behavior such as drawing a line, instead of writing out a bunch of code, all you need to do is call the function. But sometimes you would like to choose different behaviors at different times in essentially the same piece of code.

Example: int (*fp) (int, int); -> Function pointer returning an integer

8.12 Size of Datatypes

Name	Description	Size*	Range*
char	Character or small integer.	1byte	signed: -128 to 127 unsigned: 0 to 255
short	Short Integer.	2bytes	signed: -32768

int (short)			to 32767 unsigned: 0 to 65535
int	Integer.	4bytes	signed: -2147483648 to 2147483647 unsigned: 0 to 4294967295
long int (long)	Long integer.	4bytes	signed: -2147483648 to 2147483647 unsigned: 0 to 4294967295
bool	Boolean value. It can take one of two values: true or false.	1byte	true or false
float	Floating point number.	4bytes	+/- 3.4e +/- 38 (~7 digits)
double	Double precision floating point number.	8bytes	+/- 1.7e +/- 308 (~15 digits)
long double	Long double precision floating point number.	8bytes	+/- 1.7e +/- 308 (~15 digits)

8.13 What is the difference between typedef & Macros?

Typedef is used to create a new name to an already existing data type. Redefine the name creates conflict with the previous declaration.

eg:
typedef unsigned int UINT32

Macros [#define] is a direct substitution of the text before compiling the whole code. In the given example, its just a textual substitution. where there is a possibility of redefining the macro eg:

```
#define chPointer  char *
#undef chPointer
#define chPointer int *
```

Typedef are used for declarations when compare with macro
typedefs can correctly encode pointer types.where as #DEFINES are just replacements done by the preprocessor.
For example,

```
typedef char *String_t;
#define String_d char *
String_t s1, s2; String_d s3, s4;
```

s1, s2, and s3 are all declared as char *, but s4 is declared as a char, which is probably not the intention.

8.14 What is the difference between a macro and a function?

Macros are essentially shorthand representations of arbitrary sections of the source code, which makes the source code, while its (the macro template's) expansion replaces each of its presence prior to compilation. Whatever is there to do with Macros, it is done by the preprocessor, so that the source code is ready for compilation. Function is a calling routine, whence a large program is divided into separate portions, each portion doing a separate job, and proper calling of these portions in different places combines the works done by them into the required complete output.

Thus functions have nothing to do with the preprocessing period, they are just compiled. To some extent function and macro is similar, for a macro can occasionally be invoked to perform a task that is generally entrusted to a function. But the similarity ends there.

The differences are:

1. Macro consumes less time. When a function is called, arguments have to be passed to it, those arguments are accepted by corresponding dummy variables in the function, they are processed, and finally the function returns a value that is assigned to a variable (except for a void function). If a function is invoked a number of times, the times add up, and compilation is delayed. On the other hand, the macro expansion had already taken place and replaced each occurrence of the macro in the source code before the source code starts compiling, so it requires no additional time to execute.
2. Function consumes less memory. While a function replete with macros may look succinct on surface, prior to compilation, all the macro-presences are replaced by their corresponding macro expansions, which consumes considerable memory. On the other hand, even if a function is invoked 100 times, it still occupies the same space. Hence function is more amenable to less memory requirements.

8.15 What is inline function?

Inline function is the optimization technique used by the compilers. One can simply prepend inline keyword to function prototype to make a function inline. Inline function instruct compiler to insert complete body of the function wherever that function got used in code.

Advantages:-
1) It does not require function calling overhead.
2) It also save overhead of variables push/pop on the stack, while function calling.
3) It also save overhead of return call from a function.
4) It increases locality of reference by utilizing instruction cache.
5) After in-lining compiler can also apply intraprocedural optmization if specified. This is the most important one, in this way

compiler can now focus on dead code elimination, can give more stress on branch prediction, induction variable elimination etc..

Disadvantages :-

1) May increase function size so that it may not fit on the cache, causing lots of cahce miss.
2) After in-lining function if variables number which are going to use register increases than they may create overhead on register variable resource utilization.
3) It may cause compilation overhead as if some body changes code inside inline function than all calling location will also be compiled.
4) If used in header file, it will make your header file size large and may also make it unreadable.
5) If somebody used too many inline function resultant in a larger code size than it may cause thrashing in memory. More and more number of page fault bringing down your program performance.
6) Its not useful for embeded system where large binary size is not preferred at all due to memory size constraints

8.16 What is the difference between a macro and a inline function?

Macros :

1. input argument datatype checking can't be done.
2. compiler has no idea about macros
3. Code is not readable
4. macros are always expanded or replaced during preprocessing, hence code size is more.
5. macro can't return.

Inline function :

1. input argument datatype can be done.
2. compiler knows about inline functions.
3. code is readable
4. inline functions are may not be expanded always
5. can return.

8.17 Preprocessor Statements #ifdef, #else, #endif

These provide a rapid way to "clip" out and insert code.

```
#define FIRST

main()

{

int a, b, c;

#ifdef FIRST

    a=2; b=6; c=4;

#else

    printf("Enter a:");

    scanf("%d", &a);

    printf("Enter a:");

    scanf("%d", &a);

    printf("Enter a:");

    scanf("%d", &a);

#endif
```

Note that if FIRST is defined (which it is in the above) the values of a, b and c are hardcoded to values of 2, 6 and 4. This can save a lot of time when developing software as it avoids tediously typing everything in each and everytime you run your routine. When FIRST is defined, all that is passed to the compiler is the code between the #ifdef and the #else. The code between the #else and the #endif is not seen by the compiler. It is as if it were all a comment.

Once you have your routine working, and desire to insert the printf and scanfs, all that is required is to go back and delete the the #define FIRST. Now, the compiler does not see the;

a=2; b=6; c=4;

8.18 Swap 2 variables without using temporary variable:

$a = a + b$

$b = a - b$

$a = a - b$

8.19 Write a program to generate the Fibonacci Series?

```
#include<stdio.h>

#include<conio.h>

main()

{

int n,i,c,a=0,b=1;
```

```
printf("Enter Fibonacci series of nth term : ");

scanf("%d",&n);

printf("%d %d ",a,b);

for(i=0;i<=(n-3);i++)

{

c=a+b;

a=b;

b=c;

printf("%d ",c);

}

getch();

}Output :

Enter Fibonacci series of nth term : 7

0 1 1 2 3 5 8
```

8.20 Write a program to find unique numbers in an array?

```
for (i=1;i<=array.length;i++) {

found=false;

for (k=i+1;k<=array.length;k++) {

if (array[i]==array[k]) found=true;

}

if (!found) println(array[i]);

}
```

8.21 Write a C program to print Equilateral Triangle using numbers?

```
#include<stdio.h>

main()

{

    int i,j,k,n;
```

```
printf("Enter number of rows  of the triangle \n");

scanf("%d",&n);



for(i=1;i<=n;i++)

{

        for(j=1;j<=n-i;j++)

        {

                printf(" ");

        }

        for(k=1;k<=(2*i)-1;k++)

        {

                printf("i");

        }

        printf("\n");

}

getch();
```

***********End of Book****************************

28207715R00048

Printed in Great Britain
by Amazon